More Advance Praise for Key Bridge

"Despite Rumble's wry protestation of being 'safe in sound' this book ranges magnificently from its cell. At once the journal of two-plus bad years in Babylon, a psychic geography of D.C. and its implications, and a blistering investigation of the unstableness of color-as-metaphor Ken Rumble's *Bridge* is, finally, a great deal more than some ceremonial key to a fabled city—this key gifts its recipient with unlikely knowledge. *Key Bridge* is a book of exceptions, a close telling of jeopardies and penchants, a gift of directions." —C. S. GISCOMBE

"An ambitious study of polis, power, and memory, Ken Rumble's *Key Bridge* weaves together private and public history. A native and naïve voice emerges from this geo-poetical landscape, raising candid questions about the bridges that we cross and the troubled waters around us." —LISA JARNOT

"D.C. bleeding shot by shot? D.C. as waiting room for its own rebirth? Ken Rumble's *Key Bridge*—a reanimation, retrieval and investigation of his native city—thrillingly initiates the heroic endeavor to 'write what's gone': punk buttons, sex in parking lots, shadow names, B-movie dreams, the mystery of the D.C. sniper(s), 'a dream of the city.'

But what city? The city where the speaker 'learned / the way to sound'? The first 'chocolate city'? The city of 'when I was one / on hopes for unannounced Fugazi'? The city where Francis Scott's home was 'demolished,/ demolitioned, & generally destroyed / for the bridge that bears his name'?

Clearly, it is now Rumble's city. Section by section, the strange distance between D.C.'s official histories and its unofficial street life becomes the space in which the poem continually returns to invent the terms by which 'this sinking, swamp built city' can momentarily reveal itself to be something else: a forest, or a thrift shop, or a saucer the speaker spins in order to 'see how it loves.'"
—TONY TOST

Key Bridge

Ken Rumble

Carolina Wren Press
Durham, North Carolina

Design: Lesley Landis Designs
Cover Image: Historic American Engineering Record, Francis Scott Key
   Bridge, aerial view looking north. Photograph by Jack Boucher, 1972.
Cover decorative border: Map © by Rand McNally, R.L.07-S-08

*The mission of Carolina Wren Press is to seek out, nurture, and promote
literary work by new and underrepresented writers, including women
and writers of color. We gratefully acknowledge the ongoing support made
possible through gifts to the Durham Arts Council's United Arts Fund.*

Library of Congress Cataloguing-in-Publication Data
Rumble, Ken, 1974–
  Key Bridge / Ken Rumble
  p. cm.
ISBN 978-0-932112-54-5
I. Title

PS3618.U565K49 2007
811'.6-dc22

200700738

I would like to thank the editors of the following journals for publishing the following sections:

Parakeet: "13.march.2002"
VeRT: "15.june.2000"
Fascicle: "18.june.2002"
New College Review: "4.march.2001," "24.january.2002," "1.october.2002"
Octopus: "25.december.2000," "28.december.2000"
Moria: "20.august.2002"
Coconut: "12.april.2002," "8.october.2002," "31.october.2002"
Gutcult: "3.october.2002," "2.september.2001," "4.april.2002"
Typo: "18.may.2000"
Cutbank: "21.january.2003," "28.march.2001," "10.april.2001," "9.april.2002"
MiPoesias: "30.april.2002"
Talisman: "9.january.2003"
can we have our ball back?: "5.march.2002"
Wherever We Put Our Hats: "14.july.2002," "28.november.2002," "21.november.2002," "15.january.2002," "17.january.2002"
Xconnect: "31.december.2002," "17.march.2001," "12.august.2001"
Drunken Boat: "31.january.2002," "14.february.2002"
Carolina Quarterly: "16.may.2000," "17.december.2000," "26.may.2000"
Word For Word: "15.may.2000," "18.march.2001"
Cranky: "1.april.2001"
The North Carolina Arts Council's Poet of the Week Project (11/21/05 – 11/27/05): "3.august.2001," "8.september.2001"

Many, many thanks also to Mom & Dad, Heather, Ann & Co, Lili, Jim & Charlotte, Evie, Tessa, Debbie, Andrea, Chris, Todd, Tony, Brian, Marcus, Julian, Joe, David, Standard, Patrick, Randall, Adam, past, present & future members of the Lucifer Poetics Group & the guests of the Desert City: your hearts beat poetry.

with love to
Violet, Cecil & Lori

A Way In

Let me see your beauty broken down,
like you would do for one you love.
—*Leonard Cohen*

The problem is how to we all
together now.
—*Juliana Spahr*

Key Bridge

breath.   )
Now   )

15.may.2000

D.C. city light crests on lampposts
ripples through streets
ripples through buildings
through trees
through cars
through clothes
ripples through you   (river

Think of this: (beside
her name's Jenny, blond, doesn't
like sex in bed, fell for you
at a party on lines like fish—
her thin cotton dress
in ruffles on your belly

Down the hill from the corner lot
the Potomac silent & large like thought
        (*Patowmack* the old map reads
        (not *it*, me.
Traffic turns from the bridge
into Georgetown right *there*—

Jenny says *fuck me* & you say, of course,
please, paper white you say *please,*
without regard
for the D.C. blue,
white, or black—the police are an island
you can choose not to visit,

1

not walking through
the night's blue hours alone,
not speeding on Whitehurst full of dope,
not stealing, not lying, not laughing
about it all, with nothing
like worry, not here, *please,*
fucking a woman the color of strawberries in ice
in an empty lot at the west end of Georgetown
not here would you think
that if seen & black
what a difference that'd make.

—

Awake & it's 5 a.m. &
the light again. We (meaning me & who
walk through the sinking fog
to the bridge to yell *Go!*
to the misty crew teams
practicing in the river below.
We watch the city breathe in
the yellow shining fog.

This sinking, swamp-built city
concrete city, cherry tree city, newspaper city
the wind in
like loose fish.

(a river

Here we put the name before the thing:
Mississippi River, Snake River, Post Pond, Potomac River

There it's the reverse:
River Thames, River Liffey, Loch Ness,
        Loch Lough, River Cam.

16.may.2000

(aerial view

way far from D.C. & way below, a river winds
        through a pancake middle
                state like audio tape
                        off the reel—wherever rivers
                            wind the same
                                    song the same

—

This is an entrance, a door jamb
from which to survey the room.

Here, three hundred feet above the river, the shores,
the blue water

always undulates
hips, boat. *Here*

is a place for a trance

(city in a city without *the City*

—

Celebrate & Discover

—

South of the river Rosslyn rises,
Northern edge of Northern
Virginia. Its buildings break
the limit, the capital level
restriction. D.C.'s south edge returned to Virginia
in 1846—it had nothing to do
with the Civil War.

3

Another Jenny lived there
long, dark red hair, skin like a running river.

With her once when day ended
in Rosslyn—day's end empties
Rosslyn—alone in an empty city we
looked after dark

—

Trips downtown with my parents & sister in
from the suburbs through Rock Creek Park (the *scenic* route
to see museums, past packs
of spangled flat-back cyclists, we turn
from the park road at the river by Thompson's Boathouse,
we turn down Virginia past Watergate (in the city now
my sister & I watch for bums
on steam grates, we call out
& point when we see them,
I thought they were called *bombs* &
didn't understand how people
could explode.

18.may.2000

The last bridge to Virginia within city limits
Georgetown's end: streets
store fronts sidewalks slide
into unruly
city forest
& go
       (opposite Anacostia

The bridge to 66 & NoVa suburbs,
traffic's push-me-pull full
of Saab, Lexus, Benz & red
red flashing. *Getting out of this*
city's always
difficult.

—

          (others:
pause,
entrance, no
place exists only crossed
only a minute—only
notable in traffic reports
(*whup,* (*whup,* (*whup*
(the heli-
      copter

Around the bridge is
moving, bridge
still.

24.may.2000

Southeast: Value City thrift store (best in town
dangerous [   ] place
me & the beige black & white photographer
looked for castoffs:
polyester, big collared, blue, leopard print,
plaid, busy, black, denim, untied, with tulips,
vinyl, white, thick, striped,
paisleys, moons, rayon, *Sergio,* red—

the photographer could hardly move her arms.
It being a working day—us skipping school—
few heads bobbed among
the second hand racks of second
hands. I found a mechanic's shirt with *Raj*
in cursive
above the pocket
          (*cool, man*

26.may.2000

the blossoms
fall it
feels as if
walking
underwater petals

—

(don't tell stories

yellowish light from lights:
neon, street, car, signal, store: a meniscus
between the building tops—
        (streets as *tracks for light,* a recess where light
          (could be inlaid

A bar door opens like a canal lock, music
washes out on the street, a camel-colored couple
washes out on the sidewalk, washes &
ricochets between buildings
up &
beyond: curly tree tops,
then nothing
where the river
is

beyond the river, black below
the tree tops

(again)
buildings & light yellow
like sandy Mall pathways
        (a green hose curving people into the city

—

Memorial Bridge where the marathon runners flow over &
down & into the city from Arlington's hill & tombstones

Memorial Bridge's wide low arches
stand on water

4.june.2000

An other, an out there, away

6.june.2000

A low brick tower
with turrets
in the middle of the Northwest
suburbs atop the hill end
of Fort Reno Park
a few blocks
from Hechinger's Hardware

Summer nights the punks come here
        (& me when I was one
on hopes for unannounced Fugazi
shows, hopes for a break
from prep school
emo bands
& their angry hopeful songs
about social
justice

—

My father led me through the hills & woods still
tangling the edges of what was extremity
& is
Northwest's suburbs.

The Civil War defensive posts
notch the hillsides, guarded, then,
against Maryland & Dixie both

        (John Wilkes Booth knew the way
                (regardless

—

Coming up, if I'd said the "N-word"
my parents
—liberal, kind, pale
as book pages, freckly, Catholic,
love Cézanne—
would've made me pray.

13.june.2000

A city, *A Capital City* where
my hay-skinned, southern grandmother stumbled,
      split her chin, where
I circled the mastodon in the Museum of
      Natural History, where
I cast a hundred-foot shadow on the National Cathedral, where
my mother drove me to get punk buttons
      from the punk store, where
I drank so much coffee I saw Tonto crouched
      on the ceiling, where
I crossed each acid state & bombs burst, where
I learned
the way to sound.

—

To me, in these places, white people have said:
in Georgetown: *He mess with me I'll hang him on a tree* &
in Cleveland Park: *You can shoot them around here,*
just first tell the cops
he's been messing with you &
on East Capitol: *Look at that dumb nigger* &
in Federal Triangle: *I hate niggers period. Sand niggers, black*
niggers, blue niggers, yellow niggers, red niggers,
all of them &
all over the place: white people look at me
when they don't say *nigger*

[14.january.2003

Lee Boyd Malvo—shooting star
I was never going to be like you.
      (my life was below your trajectory

        (*Number one with a bullet*

Not even a metaphor
for death
but death
itself.

John Allen Muhammad
      (you loved someone
      (someone loved you

John Lee, a boy who did a man's crime
John Allen, are you one? two? lovers?
      (*queer* some say in whispers
      (the *queer* adding distance
      (extending the light years of distance between
      (how unfathomable you both are, John

two? one?
NASA won't find you
but distance is
your talent:
      (distance & (disintegration

black, Muslim, a child & a veteran
one? two?

symbiotic: an extension
of your arm, *point*
& squeeze
two? one?

you loved someone & were loved maybe by many
but you are

we will kill you]

15.june.2000

                                        luminous   translucent
                              illuminant   luminary   dazzling
                         bright   shining   burning
                   glowing   twinkling   gleaming
            incandescent   sparkling   transparent
         burning   city   flickering
   city   flickering city
of angles

The city is a bowl spilling *now*
         Every person here is still
                  here The buildings
                           overlap in exposure People
                                    pass through people
                                             who pass people
                  From above, the city
                           shifts like gasoline in a puddle
                                    a chess game sped
                                             into lines

[15.december.2002

the way linked moments separated by time become

consecutive—the space between disappears, reappears, dis-
         appoints

spooky]

17.june.2000

write what's gone

20.june.2000

Teardrops, wood, an eye:
these have nothing to do
with D.C.

the public D.C., the showy D.C., the show-me D.C.,
D.C.'s pubs & undergrounds
these have nothing to do
with the District of
Columbia

The insistent ring of a telephone:
tell me, will you, how big the earth?
the span of my reach? who governs
the city?

Put your money
in the weight guesser
Tell a friend
how round they are

There is only will.

7.december.2000

Further away

What did he do weekends
while I turned my head into a bowl
to keep my goldfish straight?
He said he kept turtles about,
had two tanks with several kinds.

[24.november.2002

Crime
        bespeaks
                a benighted
                        presence]

17.december.2000

Back

Diamond city, follow
angles, facets—some say *veins*—
to faces, agendas—
because place is a picture
of an occurrence—an avalanche
hung by film above the treeline—past
& future theories—time—
there is always time—time—even at the end—

The rookery cackles with calls
blue herons swoop in & out
like a working lung above the mouth
of the Potomac. After mating season
the herons fly solo low back up
the river inland into land into
the pools, rivers, lakes the glaciers left—
the herons' long sweep & lope with Zed necks up
the river—pull up in trees—
huddle under wings at the edge
of Roosevelt Island where
roots break the bank, turn in
to the water—herons follow the river & C&O
all the way to Ohio,
Pennsylvania, Indiana, Michigan, Wisconsin—some stay

25.december.2000

Portuguese widows
on 18th in
Adams Morgan
knit their own dark
shawls *Let me spin you*
a yarn
I say
there's only one
story:
yours.

28.december.2000

another 2000 D.C. New Year's:
I call hotels
        (the different/the same
I call restaurants
        (the same/the different
I call a cab
        (same difference

then a blue-striped taxi
        (Barwood Company suburb corpuscles
then yellow checks
        (City Co. the city now
a Ghanaian driver
        (but is he black?
then an Arab
        (wearing a turban?

If I stepped
from my body
        (black or white)
        into your body
                (black or white)
                I could watch my
                        (black or white)
                        body do this:

New Year's 1991: a hotel
on the hem of Georgetown, three friends
        (girls (not Jennys
& you
        (Linda
rent a room
        (what does narrative do
you
talk her into going down
        (what does the city
a dry hump of ink

In the B-movie dream,
Tom Waits played
the evil elf. The white-suited, white villain
turned into a sexpot,
then had trouble explaining her way
out of the vertical restaurant.
These ones worshipped dead soldiers
          who appeared in white fire
& loaned power. They found the good elf,
burned him to sketched bone—a stumbling drunk,
it wasn't hard. The skeletons in
the closet undid the villain.

          (the *trouble* with dreams is not
          (that they're not

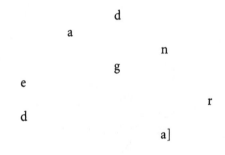

4.january.2001

(the long way through the park

Frost flecks in park grass
shine Not
stars or tears or lightning
bugs or diamonds or gods
or years loved & lost or caught
tips of Atlantic waves, eyes,
a family, souls,
dead loves,
a net catching dark, love
running light, dust.
It's the same as on the car
barring location.

9.january.2001

Heavy heavy or heavy petting.
Rubber balls I sent spinning
into heavy traffic.

12.january.2001

How a place can hold so much time

place solid time denied

City Beautiful, City of White, beautiful

D.C.: the dream the curve of

bone that is my hip I can see straight

down from the yard I cracked

my shoulder on the rooftop's inevitable

slant chimney strapped with an aerial sycamore

branches working their way in all the

way down, see can I reach there

from here through the doubled the paired

windows beneath the hood of Mr. Washington's

monument down the curved road over East-

West into Rock Creek Park that gully

of forest, green bony finger where it's been

beat back over what cathedral towers

what's missing—the road is down

the road there's the zoo the monkey

house dome, Mount Pleasant

beside the site riots, sister

Wisconsin, too—Hechinger's in

Tenley, AU, a dip

(CC circle) (dyed blue billy-

goat bridge beetle wing

colored joggers bouncing down

the path the creek through this thread

of forest trimmed distant white Meadowbrook

Stables (where the man would be (the centaur

soccer field dirt rut running from goal

to goal, open triangles point

down from the goal to where below

brown Indian head bridge look by

Thompson's Boathouse Watergate's toothy

balconies east west the hill

down Constitution there

there   there   there   there

darker prewar stone green

mealy treetops home below somewhere

dark foundation wherever you look

15.january.2001

(somewhere

She stepped in the crook of
her mother's knee,
then hip, then shoulder, then flew

       (I'm not explaining this right
Listen,
this is beautiful:
the body is a tool,
a wedge, scythe, ladder, brick, chair,
rope, shed, book, wheel, lathe, pen

—crook? the thief of her knee?
the cutpurse, skulldugger
or petty larcenist of her knee?

Minimus: two I's, no pee,
       (hard life

[31.december.2002

shadow squirrel running
        (more like wave-ing
along shadow branch
        (*to look at a landscape without describing it*
what it is—over there, out there—is a clown in a bear suit:
flat, palm out, vertical, saying
stay where you are, saying
this is the difference
between you & me: position
        (*what is position if there is no contortion?*
the *this is my side* & *that is yours*
the car's armrest down between my sister & me
the *no man's land*

but again:
shadow squirrel shadow runs
shadow life in your shadow pants
shadow arms play shadow games

shadow names give shadows aim
water's shadow like shadow's shadow
shadow day like shadow gaze

shadows talk & shadow stalk
shadows mock & move like us
long for the beginning of night like us

shadow is what it holds
isn't gone when it goes
shadows talk on shadow talk
        (*what evil lurks in the hearts of men*
don't leave where they've left
        (*this shadowy thing, this skin*
shadow's show, breath, reach
        (*How that dream faded & began*
        (*to revive eighty years later.*
shadow's orbit shadow orbits

—the fixed position]

4.february.2001

D.C. night: my head against the car window
(bumps & potholes
feeling more than seeing
the purple-orange algorithm
of street lamps like blips across
a heart monitor—a music I feel
more than hear, a cardiology I imagine
more than see

20.february.2001

I have to get groceries
to cook dinner
to balance my checkbook
but here I am on my couch
watching a streetlight
writing about people

the scent of them like apples & sheep
their mouths mooning into smiles
their bodies an organ of touch
that there is so much space
around where bodies
could be.

The streetlight fills my room now
not it but its light
not my room
but my bone room
not there
but my mind's range out still

where there are so many people.

[11.december.2002

(*un beso de luna* traveling to find one

—

Silver Spring: *is there a problem with crime?*
Northeast: *oh, it's sketchy*
Anacostia: *that place is scary*
Southeast: *you don't want to be there at night*
Capitol Hill: *it's dangerous*
Capitol Heights: *Section 8*
Mount Pleasant: *in a few years this neighborhood will be great*
Adams Morgan: *it's scenic*
Takoma Park: *these are some great fixer-upper homes*

—

His name's Amos, but I'm not Andy
We jive talk about *whitey, crackers, honkies,*
call each other *muthahfuckah,* talk about *revolution*
& bringing *down the man*
But we're not Amos & Andy, but we
slap each other five & say *word up,*
homie, play the dozens on each other's mother,
talk about how we're *pimping*
But we're not Amos & Andy, but we
say *cuz,* call each other *dawg,*
Kick it with the homeboys sometimes,
sprinkle our *raps* with *yo*
But we're not Amos & Andy, but we but
    we are is white folks
        in the white space

        (snow, sunflower, sunset
        (wood grain, translucent, fall]

27.february.2001

I'm so hungover
I could eat a live cat
& feel
better.

17.march.2001

Is a bridge really like any other thing than its self?
Does calling it a *doorjamb* or a *beginning*
deny the intrinsic uniquity of the bridge?

Dear Metaphor,
        you amoebae; you gumwad; you not-so-fresh feeling; you
soap that is not clean; you toffee in the back molar; you smoky
room; you debate; you air; you diarrhea on horseback; you super-
market cactus; you squid-eating squid; you floss; you sponge; you
bag of colored thumbtacks; you dust; you having it your way; you
front of the class; you coil; you little miss; you standing by the sink
eating crackers; you empty ice cube tray still in the freezer; you

—

Key Bridge—named after
Francis Scott Key of *rockets' red glare* fame—
was originally an aqueduct bridge,
a bridge of water over water. Odd,
but odd enough to mean anything.
Some merchants wanted to get canal boats
from the C&O across the Potomac into Fairfax
where the tariffs were lower
than in the port town of Georgetown
where Thompson's Boathouse
still occupies space & time
but didn't then.

(bridge, bridged, bridgey

18.march.2001

the bridge bridged the bridgeable river,
bridgely bridging the bridged river

Bridge is. It is.
The bridge exists, is exits,
exists/is, is ex-
the bridge occupies,
colonizes, engages, conquers, invades, seizes,
maintains, captures, pervades, takes over, storms,
grasps, extends, is

time & space—
indivisible time, space & form: the bridge:
the fluid form of intangibilities. The
bridge is.
Bridge be.
Bridge be bridging.

28.march.2001

Washington D.C. & Vicinity
   Inside the Beltway

Spread flat & colored Pierre L'Enfant's city
plan clarifies like lemon writing:
my fractured
& monstrous diamond:

perpendicular streets graph the interior
blue boulevard lines angle through
converge into circles
beam out again to the city limits
like webs veins cracked slate
palm lines palm fronds roots ant lines

[7.november.2002

memory becomes
memory like a cold, like
a splinter,
& then a memory
memory

your memory is that,
my memory is that
without, like any
          (disconservation]

1.april.2001

The bathroom door opens roiling out steam
& my mother half-naked passed
the TV screen to her room then
back again with a towel.

Then my dad hot-steps by me
half-dressed on the to & fro in
steam & Old Spice.
I do my best to ignore
those bodies that made me grow angry

at the interruption of the show the indignity
of their parade.
Then they emerge all black & white
& glittering & I ignore them as they
stand in front of the TV
kiss me & wish me *goodnight. MOVE*
I say &
they're gone.

I watch shows with guns & cars
until my eyes shut. Then awake asleep
against my dad's wool coat
on the way to bed. He passes me to my mother
to lay under the covers there
I'm in the midst of their scents their wool
& velvet lost
in their there—

        (how we are born many times
        (how we have so many parents

things:
clothes, surface, changeable

through the skin
        (in
until organs

8.april.2001

Lake Artemisia
blue bubbles, map's bladders—
mouth of Anacostia River,
way up & out
      (out out (damned spot
in Maryland:
in the loop, the ring
I-495.
Off most *D.C.*
     (meaning federal
maps, that lake drains down
        (Artemisia—genus of plants distinguished by a
        (peculiarly bitter or aromatic taste, including the
        (common wormwood, mugwort & southernwood
        (Artemis—Diana, huntress goddess of the moon
          (what do these things concern
             (with a depression in the land
               (water pools into,
                  a location (ripples
follows a ragged wave of green down
the map past Brentwood, Colman Manor, Sheverly & on
into the District, widening under Benning,
Sousa, Douglass & 11th Street Bridge, carves D.C.
to a pair of barbs where it mingles
with the Potomac loses its name mixes
spills down with the wide Potomac down
off the map into the room silt & minnows slosh
across the hardwood floors dirty pants swirl
in the slight current the bed goes dark & wet
cools knees laps ribs swells
books like bellies sweeps the page ink into faint
black clouds wets beard eyes ears breath
buoyant enough to float
a few feet off the floor

10.april.2001

Standing in the mirror
standing in, the mirror
                (which comes from *mere*
                ((which means *lake*
                (((which are fed by or feed
                ((((mouths of rivers

In a dream a model landscape & tower:
a river lifted away in a piece
like drapes

7.june.2001

Oooh, where is my city now that I need it?
In a new home crowded
by boxes, the Metro Center of love,
that esophageal chamber—honeycomb
of beige cement—whooshing
its trains in & out, whooshing
their doors open & closed, whooshing with the bing
bong bell, whooshing ochre tiles
marking paths like what.

9.june.2001

(just outside the District

Three men sit, feet propped level
with their buckles—kitchenlight
pushes into the porch like a postman
There's a joke they know

       (that we recognize each other by
       (instinct, impulse, gravity

[20.december.2002

The monster: sight, vision, rays & paths: light beams

The monster:
nothing but *here* obsessed.

> (*Why where I was & what I was*
> (*doing at the time matters.*

The monster: not a wolfman, more inhuman
                    on the outside, more
human in—the inter-

D.C.'s light
beams
the monster.]

18.june.2001

*Although the city has retained some aspects of its Southern origin, it has
assumed a much more cosmopolitan character.*

> (regret the *rednecks*

*Partly because the city was originally formed from slave-holding states,
the national capital has always had a significant black presence.*

> (present the *absence*

*Southern—adj. 1. Of persons: living or originating in, coming from, the
south, esp. of Great Britain, England, or of Europe.*

> (Britain's northern *rednecks*
> (London is *cosmopolitan*

23.june.2001

There's more evidence than words
    (worlds

24.june.2001

Washington, District of Columbia: A place,
an area marked, walked,
photographed, drawn & reproduced

not going anywhere, not
to the supermarket,
to the tanning bed, not

to vote, not
to worship, not to step outside
for a smoke: I cannot follow
it anywhere, watch it & scribble notes

in a spiral pad, stop to trip my hands
over fruit to watch the city
chat in the supermarket
about appropriate potatoes.

Geography's motion is solar, galactic, universal,
on the level of the city, frenetic & static
gray water boiling in a pot
worms tangling in spare dirt at
the bottom of a cup
legless no

destination save time it's not going
anywhere it's not going nowhere
it's going it's not going
it's going it's

It's going to be here
along time.

26.june.2001

There are answers
but they are complicated answers.
There are tables like cadavers
but they are metal-legged tables.
There is history
but it is temporary.

There is a hill like so:
        (NE Georgia Ave.—
driving into the city, reaching
the top of this hill, open your eyes, yes,
look ahead & right, don't speed,
don't speed, look, see,
open your eyes, yes,
to the city laid out
like directions.

29.june.2001

1957: D.C. is found
        (*by whom?* (a white guy probably (as if he lost it
        (white guy: *aww shit, honey? where'd I put that*
        (*goddamn city now? Let's see:*
        (*keys, wallet, toothbrush, I walked into the den,*
        (*turned on the tube, turned to say*
        (*hello*
to have the first black majority
in a major U.S. city.
Chocolate city.
D. Chocolate City: the first one.

*Until recently, the great majority of the black population was located inside
the city. But like an earlier generation of whites, the black middle class
began to leave the city & move to the suburbs.*
        (white fright

3.august.2001

(Friday, 9:32 pm, October
I'm 17, peach light, Matt stops the car
under the red & white Kentucky Fried Chicken sign
just over the border on the corner of Georgia & Alaska

halfway down the block, we pass the bums who know what
we know about the Chinese take-out place
with bulletproof glass

there's a party somewhere
somewhere, there's a party
somewhere, somebody's parents went somewhere else
& somebody isn't being watched by somebody
like they ought to be being watched

there's a party somewhere
somewhere there's a party
somewhere

12.august.2001

the only motion is circular
not cycles but circles
turning like checkbooks taken like
school boys frightened like anatomy

there is land before the poem
a vista that pulls away from touch:
a blue-lettered showgirl

2.september.2001

*—Why do you think you & other African American tenors have had a hard
time breaking into the opera world?*
—Because the tenors get the girl.

monochrome, monoculture, monotone,
mononucleosis, mano y mano y no hermana o hermano

—

Ahh, my city, today I missed you
where I would've gone?
you're a nest to me always next to me
a palm a mind a diamond—I'd walk
the streets I drive the desk down
like in the movie I don't remember the name of.
Even your rats tumbling over each other along
the footpath along
the Potomac a long
ways
away.

—

Don't be *delicate.*
Use a whip,
a note, a rhythm, or *not*

3.september.2001

Pierre L'Enfant & Ben Banneker
walked the Aves the Blvds the Sts the Rds & Circles
they drew the lives they made

saw or dreamed lives
walked & saw fountains in circles angles edges interstices

North/south the numbers go:
16th, 14th 12th, 19th
east/west the letters:
N, P, F, S, M, U
then two-syllable names alphabetically:
Fuller, Girard, Irving, Quincy

then three syllables:
Allison, Delafield, Jonquil, Rittenhouse—all by alphabet
up to the north tip
          (spent *rage for order*
until the pattern is left in a tangle
of Redwood Spruce Sycamore Tulip & Tamarack
          (before that: Arcadia

the Capitol building
          (slave-built
the center the Cyclops's eye
my dear dear little monster:
this balance this grid slashed
NE/SE with state names, this monster
geometry

dreamed into swamp land
L'Enfant & Banneker walked through
seeing city all around not

the web the veins the branches not
the swamp the fractured glass not
the palm lines not the spokes the city

the city, the city, seeing all
about
the city.

8.september.2001

Here's the story: his name's Frank
in my English & drama classes, second-period lunch,

the only black invitee to my 13th birthday
showed up an hour early

he'd ridden the bus
from his apartment complex

we ate pizza, watched *Night of the Living Dead*,
Day of the Dead & *Dawn of the Dead*—movies

about race.

15.september.2001

I know nothing
even about my city
my wounded angel
my paramour my geometry
I've been so long for you

Where am I? Where am I now?
trying to clasp the whole
          (all of you, all of us
to love the broken enough

24.december.2001

The return from there from her
Park Road above the park
blue weight & location
blue 3 a.m. Tuesday taxis—she that
she there
            (she *all* that
good-ness visions sake slakes
there, above the zoo
            (the zoo
the giraffe & elephant
            (what?
the city & she
name, history & stake
a stake in the world
an open hand there,
an open hand curled into the sign
for *brick* for *sun* for *height* for *here* for *land*
for *land* for this we
know: ether & the angles:
this woman this city this coincidence this concordance
this conjunction this freedom this injunction
to call you in this first hour of this 27th Christmas

[28.november.2002

Cold Thanksgiving, still all

tomatoes won't grow now, but we thank them

Thanksgiving: the question being:
to whom? & (of course) where?

I thank you: Amos, Violet, Heather, Mom, Dad, Ann, Johnnie Mae, Lili

the place of giving
the place to which
something is given
a receiver something still,
out of the movement
              they say *the universe ends when it stops*

Cecil, Jim, Charlotte, Robin, Robin, Lyrae, Matthew

              they say that *stars orbit each other*
              that looking out (away) into the dark & light
              of the night
              that looking out from the city (or what have you
              that looking at this sky & seeing two near stars
              paired, pinpricks of white
              in this black sky, this night & seeing these stars,
              that seeing them, the afterimage of them,
              that they could be compared, the man & his boy—
              his boy doing all the killing

orbits & absence, the lack
              of straight lines in this
                          hyperbolic space

Hugh, Jon, Sunny, Marc, David, Evie, Lisa, Jennifer

              that *sight is a measure*, the lean
              & sway of each path—
              the *sight* as a metaphor for a path

in our sphere—binary stars
& a black man & a black boy: the far metaphor,
that *other, unknowable* metaphor
that the distance between self & object, the distance
that you measure it, the travel from light to another

stars & magazines

Jodie, Kathy, Sam, Joe, Will, Catfish, Sam, Sherry

the city left with the in & outs
the city holding you still

It's cold there today I know, cold all through
the Potomac like metal.

      (I put my thanks in Washington
      (D.C.: the ease of it all]

15.january.2002

& now that Muhammad Ali can't speak
they put him on TV three days a week.

17.january.2002

The sweep of the city laid out like feathers
even the air above the city's.

Take this take this city spin it
like a saucer see how it loves

its people see the view from New Hampshire
see what the city offers silent as red.

& what am I here?
4 a.m., driving home without a job?

24.january.2002

(meanwhile in 1874:

The buggy bounces as does the lamp—
the white man tells the driver *16th & K*,
chuckles considering Hillary as a pineapple of reason,
fingers the key & the castle & the senate in his way.

Beside the river, she tucks a Lincoln in her pocket:
the line is the reflecting pool. *M & 4th, crappie!*
Boots filled with water, she reels out a flopping flounder,
tosses the Lincoln in the drink,
Georgetown, baby, Georgetown.

31.january.2002

The view that the world is contained in a line,
that each string is a series of worlds
held together by a force like light

that each object is & within a fractal

(d(i(s(t(a(n(c(e(

The view that the river will carry every-
thing before time's end
that there's no river at all even

that *river* is not a noun, is a verb like *smoke/land/place*

The view that metaphor can make anything anything

that metaphor can
the metaphor can

—

That view that you get from the river
of Georgetown buildings climbing feet on heads
from the bank up the hill to the National Cathedral's peaks—

13.february.2002

I say *cocks* because
I'm white apparently
black men say *dicks*

—

The clock's potential
count & measure
repeat—
repeat—
            (time's potential time's square time's cube—

14.february.2002

We came up out of the Metro at Westmoreland Circle—
sunlight fell wrapped in gauze & heavy as film sunlight
fell on the crowd & cars passing
       like the carriage of a typewriter—
on our way to Anacostia Amos & I were—we did not step
       into the car,
but there we were headed south—I sensed the river
       (Anacostia) beyond the row of eastern
storefronts like white symmetry—the buildings east & west
       crowded the road on the verge
of collapse—every block someone had nailed green street
       signs into the walls—the buildings ended—we
              followed
the hill down into the brown-wooded bottom land—inlets
       dipped in from the river like appendices—I looked
          back & saw what
must have been Civil War bunkers jutting from the north
       hillside like chins—I told Frank *I'll hold the wheel*—
          look back—look at that—a car swerved out
to pass coming towards us I swerved out & cursed—we
       followed the road up out of the valley into a parking
          lot stitched with grass & cracks—vans &
              trucks with missing
doors, scraped paint & hoods popped up like a patient—the
       cemetery gate an open angle—we circled the lot
          saying things like *chop shop, crack den* &
             being afraid & drove in—tomb-
stones parted the grey grass like knees in wrap-around skirts—
       the only green was evergreen & the ocean roiled
          beyond—I said *let's go* & *before they get*
          back & *this place is dangerous*

Is the natural state of a heart to be broken?

15.february.2002

(denuded
(delighted
      —we missed each other in inches

26.february.2002

                                      Losing city,
                    drinking

                        years
Pierre L'Enfant

          Blue   city
      This   blue
                  city

The city
waiting
for content.

[4.december.2002

subject's abuse
      (alleywise]

5.march.2002

Responsibility to tea, to the bag,
the leaf, the noose & its kite,
the tea totaller, the tea time, the tea cup,
the reflection, the because, the where,
the question of location, the bat,
the ball, the phone, the pornography
of the juice, the pterodactyl of Bombay,
the mmmmm, the champagne of tea,
to the water, the tap
Responsibility to a beverage
as if a pterodactyl as if more than
a mark of time—mark the time—
as if we didn't recall—
a centipede, as if a teacup (really
a coffee cup)—thicker,
chunky like chipped brick, for holding something
toxic, like an American or Brit,
like that reporter who'll never make a tea time,
as if the phone rang & the because where location
kite water juice responsibility

—

We kicked the walls from the houses
like fury—remember—like this,
like so—so many times—
watch—watch—every window,
every pane, a rock—gravel—a pile
where they pushed it into foundations—
watch—trails, bikes, dirt—watch—
we made it—nails in the gutter—
split beams & piss—kick drywall—
shit in the insulation—watch—houses—watched
building—watch—watch—now the bolt
needs tightening—
every coin on a string—

no beast lives
in the beautiful garden

13.march.2002

Dear Reader,

There is
so much to love.

There are trees to love. There are roads
to love. There is you to love. There is
me to love.

Sounds like us
even.

—

The trees have bark.
There is bark to love.
Roads meander or go diagonal.
There is meander or diagonal to love.

There is so much to love
that sounds like us.

Sounds bouncing all over
everything. The tree with its bark. The meandering
or diagonal road.

The eyes that watch the sound
be made by you or me or you
& me together & at the same
time on a road or by a tree or
by a tree by a road that
meanders then turns
diagonal.

—

There is loud to love.

—

The road that meanders after it is diagonal.

The tree that leaves fall by.

—

There are wholes to love
whether the bark, the leaves, the roots, the trunk,
whether the road, the lines, the pavement, the meander,
        the diagonal,
whether the you or I, the you & I,
whether the sound of the road bouncing all over the tree &
the tree itself to love.

—

The sound of the birds in the tree.
The song of the birds in the tree. The eyes
of the birds watching the tree, the road,
the you & the I.

—

There is road diagonal or
meandering, diagonal & meandering
past trees or no trees, past trees
with no birds & leaves, & birds
with no leaves & trees, & leaves
with no trees, & you & trees
or me, & you & me
& the sound of the passing the eyes & the sound
to watching together or apart
to love.

—

There is bark to love.
There is loud to love.

There are you & me
& you & me & the tree
& you & me & the tree & the road & the birds
& you & me & the tree & the road & the birds &
            together & apart making sounds.

—

There are places with many roads
to love near places with many trees
to love near many you
to love near many birds
to love near many me
to love near sounds like love
to love.

—

There is bark to love.

—

Rock Creek spills now out
between Thompson's Boathouse
& a white waterfront plaza still there
to the Potomac
upriver.

4.april.2002

We travel for several days.
We roll on past transport lines.
The light railway picks us up.
No one knows exactly where it lies.
& so with my pack & rifle I set out again on the way.

       (my thumb along the thin blue hour of her face

Key Bridge in D.C. at night:
grey, blue & black—
the piers sweeping from the river
an arch as an afterthought

D.C. at Key Bridge with night:
the old bridge's abutments grin like faith—
Whitehurst Freeway peels off the bridge early to drop
into Georgetown's Foggy Bottom

At night in D.C. on Key Bridge:
Woodrow willed you
a war birth
all those bridges we've loved before

Key Bridge during a D.C. night:
the right lane on Canal
a straight ride over
away
into Roslyn

D.C. under night above Key Bridge:
Francis Scott's home demolished,
demolitioned & generally destroyed
for the bridge that bears his name

All night D.C. just over Key Bridge:
1,791 feet & 6 inches of red love,
50 feet wide with 8-foot walks of red love,
space that defines space
that at night crosses (deep space

       (the (l)one toothed vampire—

9.april.2002

Ardea herodias

seven blue feet wide

the wings' slow weave

the sky

a river aerial part & parcel

seven feet of wing & silent *mostly*

their necks *Zed* or *Sed* an ambiguous

alphabet sign

the two on the card—one neck up

one neck down two-step

the flat flapper on the bookcase

seven feet wide

four feet high—river colored, river winged,

      river feathered, river beaked, river legged,

        river eyed

—

Jenny electric & avenue
Jenny a maiden with the handle of a man
Jenny loved Lebanese, fast Fatoosh
Jenny burning hair, cloud skin, leaf eyes
Jenny—*call me Jenn*—moved to Germany
Jenny wanted to, but didn't with me

Jenny a senator's daughter lived by a lake
Jenny on Roosevelt Island, Sweet's, the Commander,
      Au Pied, the Lodge
Jenny on Wisconsin, 36th, 37th, P, Prospect, 35th,
      M & the bridge
Jenny in March, May, April, February, January, June,
      19 & 92

(safe in sound

12.april.2002

You mean to love
                         bird
          love
I mean love to
                              the love tree
                    to the love road, bird,
dear bird. Love
                                              & leaf
tree   the
           road   parts
to mean love.

—

We should not be.

Here.
We should not.
Here.

We meaning
me. & you & you.

Should not. Be.

Here. I mean. Love.

Of possession. Love.

We. Do not. Belong love.
Here.

Possessing we should. Not
belong.

We here. Mean. Love.
Possess. Here.

Possessing we should. Be
not we. & here.

Love here we.
Belong possess. Here.

Love & mean.

We. Here. Mean.

Love. You & we.
Here.

Should not here. Love.

    —without a ghost of a chance

Belong.

[7.january.2003

The camellias bloom.

*Since mid-March the French engineer whom Washington persisted in calling
Langfang had been observed with measuring in the woods around Tiber or
Goose Creek*
>   (Powhatan Indians called Potomac
>   (*the river of swans:*
>   (*Cohongoronta*

L'Enfant—if he'd stayed sober—would've designed
Paterson, New Jersey
>   (girder, chord, tension rod, truss,
>   (rise, fall & restoration

Daily through the city stalks the picture of famine, L'Enfant & his dog.

Lewis's history of the first chocolate city,
vanilla suburbs—
his pumpernickel skin lightens to fall leaf at elevation,
as a topo map

"the changing nature" "the city's art"

"distinct neighborhoods"

"those who have sojourned"
"truly have lived"

"changing nature"
"along with"

"the federal triangle"
"those who have sojourned"]

18.april.2002

a whole other city: Anacostia
a whole other city: los federales
a whole in another: city

30.april.2002

cap cap
federal cap
cap cap
murder cap
cap cap
federal cap
cap cap
       cap (a cap-
ital
of its own

containment

—

In the dream here was Guantanamo Bay
(here is somewhere else
here was Gitmo bay like a green knuckle
look at the detainees look
at the detainees in green squares
one per as pearls

In the dream here was a Spanish villa
(here is somewhere else
here was a Spanish villa as you find it
a woman upside down on a table
fellating the host like blue Christmas
in another room

In the dream here was a forest
(here is somewhere else
here was the forest in fish eyes
& Banneker measuring roots
leaves crunching away as is
their ilk & inclination

In the dream here is overcast above the sightline
(here is somewhere else
here was overcast above sight
white marble, white sandstone,
white cement, black rails
& metro stops

18.june.2002

don't try to impress me
don't put on black shoes
       & call yourself *sailor*
don't take three apples
       & line them on the ledge
don't press
don't
don't lie in the bathroom
       to talk to your sister
don't build a wooden bird
       in your chest
don't expect me
don't talk to the stationery
don't
don't
don't say *I didn't warn you*
don't *here's the door, here's the steeple*
don't tell me the secret
       you told the bird
don't say *clouds* then
       deep mountain bellies
don't
don't expect me
don't

—

we & we are one
we & we & we are one

  Cool
"Disco"
  Dan
      (il miglior fabbro

(a D.C. of the mined

25.june.2002

—Discord 36—

"I am a patient boy"
"I am a patient boy"
"I wait, I wait, I wait, I wait"
"throw down your bulldog front"
"Free of suggestion"
"See me"
"Words"
"Words"
"Your hand to the wall at night"
"Tangle us, our desires"
"The water's burning"
"Right through me"

"I are one patient boy"
"until me wait for boy patient"
"moi, I wait for does not wait for"
"until me my time" "leaves to the base I"
"bulldog betrayal is quite" "bad entendement"
"why isn't my canned food free proposal base?"
"writewrite"
"to write"
"for promise"
"your hand" "writes down" "all night of you"
"our here is delivered"
"place condition confuse, look like" "see my"
"horizontal steel station"
"the box level skids"
"water, does not have the movement,
        does not have movement"
"toward the line"

white lightening, white collar, white slavery, white lies

white boy: 2. A favorite, pet, or darling boy. A term of endearment for a boy or (usually) a man.

white sale, whitefish, white bread, white caps, white wedding, white Christmas

whited: now rare or arch. 1. Covered or coated with white.

white house, white-haired, white hot, white house, white tea, white death, white people, off-white, white bred, white paternoster, white magic

white man: 1. A man clothed in white. 2. A man belonging to a race having naturally light-colored skin or complexion: chiefly applied to those of European extraction. b. US Slang: A man of honorable character such as one associates with a European (as distinguished from a Negro.)

white meat, white tail, white wash, white out, white walls, white water, white wine, white witch, white pages, white space, white paper, white power, White Mountains, egg white

White Moors: a nickname for the Genoese.

white flag, white Russian, white knight, white whale, white sands, white skin, white breasts, white-eyed, white face, white elephants, white head, white noise, white chocolate, white lies, white slavery

Tribal lore is always sacred & dangerous.

white cheddar, white buffalo, white snake, white dwarf, white flight]

14.july.2002

Red hands:
clock numbers:
the love of a city:
love for water
as a love for needles:
holding needles & water:
holding this city like a river:
like holding a river from below:
& the camera & the white shirt buttons
coming in fast before the black & the focus—
no—the hours we send out like newspaper
boats & the river:
what if we don't find love
 hat if e don't find love
 ha if e don find love
 ha if   don find lov
 ha if   do fi d lov
 ha if   o   fi lov
 ha i   o   i   lov

20.august.2002

Miss: loss lack
the location added (as it would
in the 16th
all loss & gain is location
miss: as in place (like in dodgeball (the little miss

missing the city

Time is the effect of being in one
place as opposed to another
(as if a valley is opposed to a ridge (ha

how one could miss the city when

Location supposed opposition
the lack of one & the need
of another idea's action

concentric circles slim the bull's-eye
to somewhere near Pennsylvania

—

She never knew the umbrellas
could grip her so—oh love—
their level, their canopy, they're madness

12.september.2002

I woke up
this morning
& my gas was disconnected they'd
& my phone was disconnected they'd
& I disconnected my leg
because I could

earlier in my dream I stood

1.october.2002

      (a dream of the city
      ((before the city, during the city,
      (((after, the city

In the dream, the city sees a giant
peeling pears with its teeth. *Which way
to Mobile, to Decatur?* she asks.
The giant's glowing nipples & imagist hair.

The giant is not the giant but is not. The city
carries a carpetbag he thinks is Wisconsin
& acts like a crepe.
River racing through the air,

the city tries to say *the ground*
down, down, but can't find its head.
The giant calls himself
T. Tickey & pulls a coin from his food.

On the ledge, the city sees *T*
antlike, like a satellite would,
like an album cover of the world's smallest band—
above & beneath this ledge there are others.

3.october.2002

The page-turning girl
turning pages—
does she lick her finger before
each page?
Does she love the pianist?
the cellist? the violero?
Conquered by the music
she turns & is not
conquered—
she reads & turns & is
not conquered—
the page-turning girl
the greater creator:
pale in black: the silent
motivator, motor,
wheel, piston & cam shaft,
but love?
love?
The page-turning girl loves
the future
with a tasteful part
& pearls.
She's present to need
there is no one
desire, solely need,
the creative art of reading
& love? We all
love the page-turning girl.

8.october.2002

#1 with a bullet

a constellation of chalk points

      (don't put *body-bags* in the poem

—

Live free

—

broken geometry proofs broken ideas girding space broken
angles
exponents
variables
length
width
angles

my city, my geometry, my broken, my flawed

cosine

now the gunman
one plus one equals
this geometry defining space that separates
space by definition
by focus: coarse, fine

I don't know what to say *here.*

the tragedy we make
the tragedy we are

22.october.2002

he's bleeding the city

one drop, one shot

at a time shooting, as if, at a time

not medicinally for no earthly

reason or earthly reason

all reasons are earthy

31.october.2002

there's travel *there*
in the sniper's
bullet path

it's the entrance & exit we care about
the former cleaner,
the latter lingers—

you are God, the former

They say *space is hyperbolic*
        (the Lone Ranger's saddle
        (with edges
        (an exaggerated universe
straight lines not the sure test

Malvo.

hung on the cover of *Time*

7.november.2002

You are here

is always true

except in love.

The book was designed by Lesley Landis Designs